Rudiment Grooves
for Drum Set

Rick Considine

Edited by Susan Gedutis

Rick Considine is endorsed by
Avedis Zildjian Company, Vic Firth Inc., and Gretsch Drums.

Berklee Media

Associate Vice President: Dave Kusek
Director of Content: Debbie Cavalier
Business Manager: Linda Chady Chase
Technology Manager: Mike Serio
Marketing Manager, Berkleemusic: Barry Kelly
Senior Designer: David Ehlers

Berklee Press

Senior Writer/Editor: Jonathan Feist
Writer/Editor: Susan Gedutis
Production Manager: Shawn Girsberger
Marketing Manager, Berklee Press: Jennifer Rassler
Product Marketing Manager: David Goldberg

ISBN 0-87639-009-2

1140 Boylston Street
Boston, MA 02215-3693 USA
(617) 747-2146

Visit Berklee Press Online at
www.berkleemusic.com

DISTRIBUTED BY

HAL•LEONARD®
CORPORATION
7777 W. BLUEMOUND RD. P.O. BOX 13819
MILWAUKEE, WISCONSIN 53213

Visit Hal Leonard Online at
www.halleonard.com

Printed in the United States of America by Patterson Printing
10 09 08 07 06 05 04 03   5 4 3 2 1

CONTENTS

INTRODUCTION

It's been said that in all drumming, there are only singles, doubles, and flams. All that rhythmic sophistication you hear in the playing of all drum set players is really just coming from the rudiments.

Rudiments are the drum language, a basic vocabulary of rhythms that drummers arrange and rearrange when they play grooves, solos, and fills. This book shows you how to apply them to the drum set in all styles of music. When you start combining the hands and feet, then orchestrating different parts of the rudiments between the various drums and cymbals on your set, you'll start to make music.

The accompanying CD will show you how the rudiments sound when you apply them to the drum set. Listen to the examples on that CD, and you'll discover that the rudiments are not just merely "stickings" for the hands, but are the foundation for all drum set playing.

DRUM SET NOTATION KEY

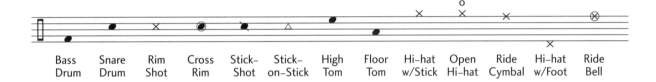

| Bass Drum | Snare Drum | Rim Shot | Cross Rim | Stick-Shot | Stick-on-Stick | High Tom | Floor Tom | Hi-hat w/Stick | Open Hi-hat | Ride Cymbal | Hi-hat w/Foot | Ride Bell |

HOW TO USE THIS BOOK

This book is made up of grooves and moves. The "grooves" are the rudiments, and the "moves" are examples of ways to play them on the drum set. Each groove is built on a particular rudiment but can be played on the drum set with any musical style, feel, or groove, and at any tempo.

Play each move first as written. Start by playing it slowly, and don't go any faster until you can play it perfectly. Only play the move faster when you can do so cleanly.

Each example can give you ideas for soloing or for drum fills, in any style. Combine different examples together to create different phrases. Use this book as an open-ended approach to developing your own creativity.

Once you can play the exercise as written, orchestrate it on the drum set. By orchestrate, I mean to play different parts of the rudiment over the various instruments in your drum set. You should orchestrate every move in the book. For all moves, the tempo and style are open, meaning that you should play them in whatever style and at whatever speed you choose.

For example, here is how a single paradiddle rudiment groove can be orchestrated into a move. The groove, or rudiment, is shown first. This is followed by the move, which shows the single paradiddle orchestrated on the drum set by replacing one of the hand parts with the bass drum.

Groove: Single Paradiddle

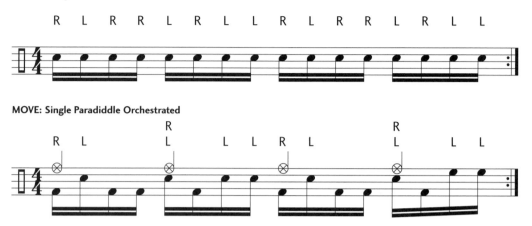

MOVE: Single Paradiddle Orchestrated

ABOUT THE CD

Every move in the book has an accompanying track on the CD. The CD tracks are for demonstration purposes only, not for play-along.

On each track, I play the move several times. The first time through, I play the move exactly as written. Then, I repeat it but orchestrate it differently on the drum set. I also may play it with a different feel. Though each repeat may sound very different, the actual rudiment I play always remains the same. Only the orchestration and the musical style change.

Listen to each demo track before you start playing each move to hear where the rudiments fit in. The CD will show you what the rudiments can sound like on a drum set, once you have the ability to control them. The examples on the CD show the way that I choose to use them; your choices may be different.

Some examples on the CD are preceded by one or two bars of time before the actual move begins. On others, I play the phrase first, then play time for a couple bars to give you a sense of a certain feel before playing time again. Use these time bars as guides for playing at the tempo and feel of your choice.

The feels and the tempos I play on the CD were purposely decided upon in the studio. When you play them, you should keep an open-minded approach to tempo, style, and orchestration as you play the moves. It is up to you to find your own way to use what I have set forth, and to choose tempos that allow you to play the moves musically.

THE 26 RUDIMENTS

These are the twenty-six basic drumming rudiments. This book will show you these rudiments can be applied to the drum set.

Make sure that you can play each of these rudiments on a single drum, such as a snare, before you attempt to orchestrate them on the drum set!

1. Single-Stroke Roll

2. Single Ratamacue

3. The Long Roll

4. Double Ratamacue

5. 5-Stroke Roll

6. Triple Ratamacue

7. 7-Stroke Roll

8. Flam Accent

9. 9-Stroke Roll

10. Flamacue

11. 10-Stroke Roll

12. Flam Tap

13. 11-Stroke Roll

14. Single Paradiddle

15. 13-Stroke Roll

16. Double Paradiddle

17. 15-Stroke Roll

18. Flam Paradiddle

19. Flam

20. Flam Paradiddle-diddle

21. Ruff

22. Drag Paradiddle No. 1

23. Single Drag

24. Drag Paradiddle No. 2

25. Double Drag

26. Lesson No. 25

SPECIFIC RUDIMENTS FOR DRUM SET

2

Listen to CD track 2, then play these from top to bottom at the same tempo. Remember to choose a tempo that allows you to play the entire exercise at the same speed.

Some of the twenty-six rudiments are more applicable to a set of drums than others. The following rudiments are among the most widely used on drum set. They transfer to the drum set very naturally.

The rudiments on their own are similar to a pianist's scales; making music with them is all about how you use them, and your motion determines your sound. To really understand the transition of rudiments to the drum set requires that you correctly phrase the inner dynamics of the rudiment. The accents you see in this example show you just one way to phrase the rudiments on drum set to make them sound more musical. It is not so much what you play, but how you sound when you play.

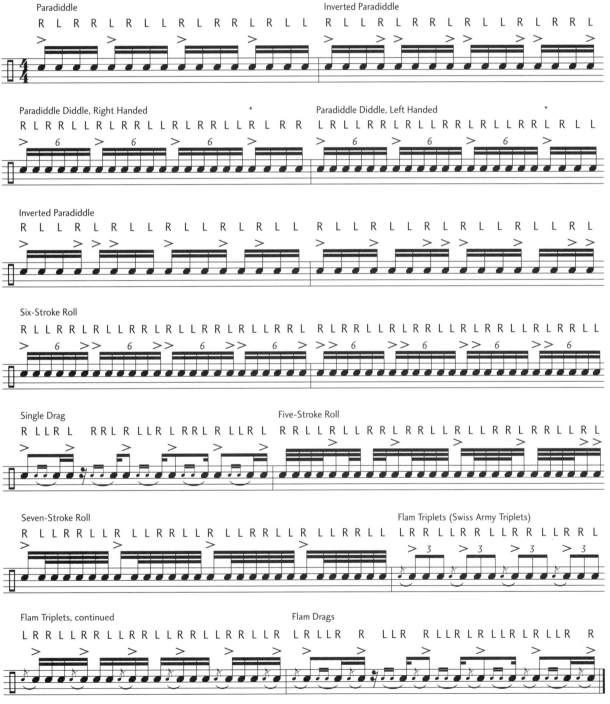

*The sixteenth note figures on beat 4 is a regular paradiddle sticking to enable you to switch hands to get the right sticking for the next figure.

APPLYING RUDIMENTS TO THE DRUM SET

The fifty grooves that follow are rudiments that you can use in your drum set playing. These grooves and moves will show you how to make the rudiments into music by your use of phrasing and accents, different rhythmic feels, and orchestration.

SECTION 1

First practice the rudiment on its own, on a single drum. Make sure that you can play it before trying to orchestrate it on the drum set.

GROOVE 1. Paradiddle Warm-up for Drum Set

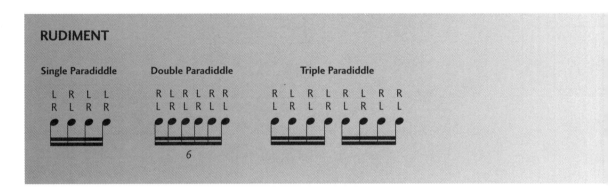

RUDIMENT

Single Paradiddle   Double Paradiddle   Triple Paradiddle

▶ MOVE

This first move is based on the paradiddle rudiment. The first four bars of this move make up a cadence that leads into the move. (A cadence is a drumming term for a short drum phrase that is played at a transition point, as an intro to a tune or as a fill.) This move will help you to recognize the inner dynamics in the rudiments when played on the drum set.

First play this warm-up move as written, at a tempo that is comfortable for you. Once you can play it perfectly from top to bottom, orchestrate the paradiddle on the drum set. Play different parts of the paradiddle rudiment on different parts of the drum set—the cowbell, the hi-hat, the ride cymbal, the toms, or any other instrument that is part of your set. Your unique sound and style as a drum set player is based on what instruments you choose and how you play them.

Play this move as written, and also try orchestrating it by substituting the snare for the closed hi-hat.

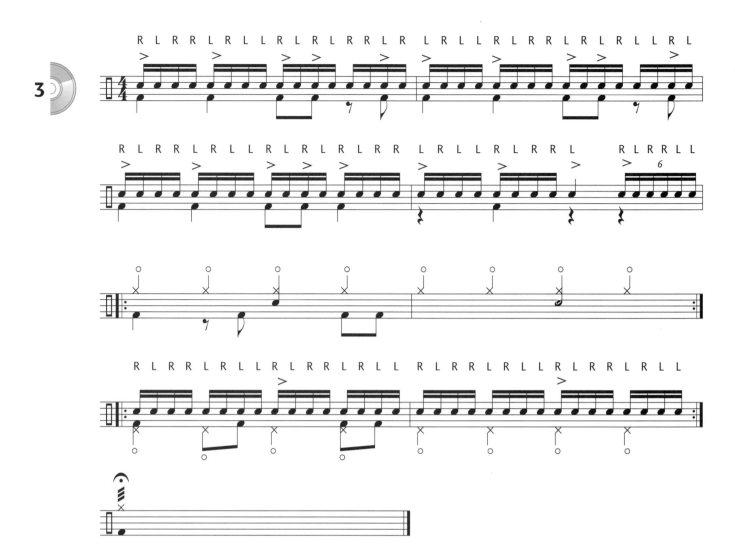

SECTION 2
SINGLE- AND DOUBLE-STROKES

Practice each rudiment on a single drum before trying to orchestrate it on the drum set.

Grooves 2 thru 6 will develop your ability to apply the rudiments to the drum set. You will work on hand/foot independence by substituting hands for feet in parts of the rudiments. These grooves will help you hear how rudiments fit into drum set playing.

GROOVE 2. Single-Stroke Roll

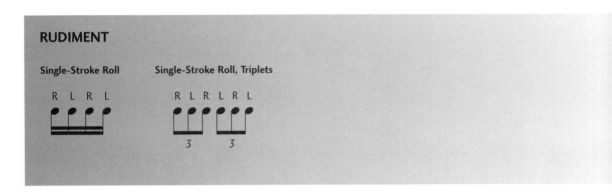

▶ MOVE

In bar 2 of this move, the bass drum substitutes for the hands in completing a part of the single-stroke roll rudiment. Play this move at a tempo that is comfortable. Then, orchestrate this single-stroke roll on the drum set. For example, play the bass drum part with the hi-hat foot instead. Or, play the snare part on the ride cymbal. Whichever instruments you choose, this move will give you practice going back and forth between playing sixteenth notes and eighth-note triplets.

When going from eighth-note triplets to sextuplets, your hands continue to play the exact same rhythm; the addition of the bass drum between the snare part creates sixteenth-note triplets.

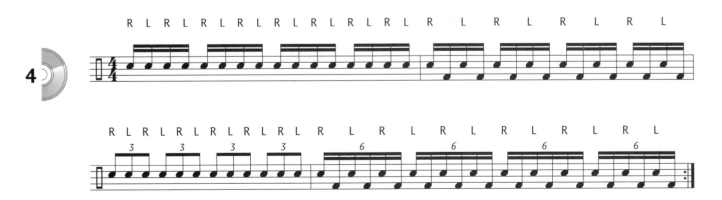

GROOVE 3. Double-Stroke Roll

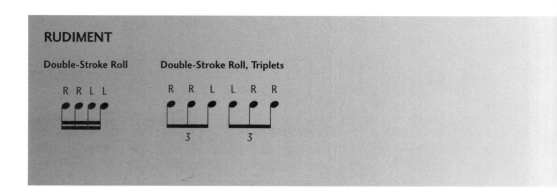

RUDIMENT

Double-Stroke Roll

R R L L

Double-Stroke Roll, Triplets

R R L L R R

▶ MOVE 1

This move illustrates a double-stroke roll played as a triplet subdivision. In this move, you'll play a triple structured roll on the snare drum, then orchestrate the double right hand on the cymbal while playing doubles on the bass drum.

▶ MOVE 2

The double-stroke roll moves the right hand between different parts of the drum set. For this and all moves, first play the phrase as written, then orchestrate it on the drum set.

▶ MOVE 3

This double-stroke roll moves the right hand between the rim of the floor tom and the rim of the snare drum. The left hand moves between the hi-hat and the rim of the snare drum.

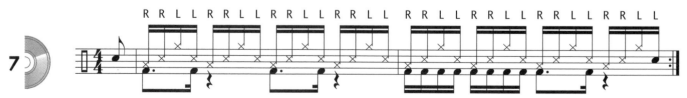

* x noteheads on the floor tom and snare should be played on the rims

GROOVE 4. Single Paradiddle and Single-Stroke Six

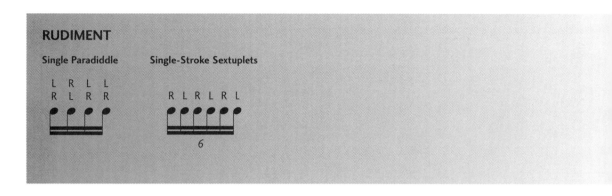

▶ MOVE

The bass drum plays the diddles. Go back and forth between sixteenth notes and sixteenth-note triplets. Alternate the hands.

GROOVE 5. Four-Stroke Ruff

▶ MOVE

In this four-stroke ruff, the left-hand part is played by the bass drum. The bass drum changes between quarter notes and eighth notes. The speed at which you can play the bass drum will determine the tempo.

GROOVE 6. Single- and Double-Stroke Triplets

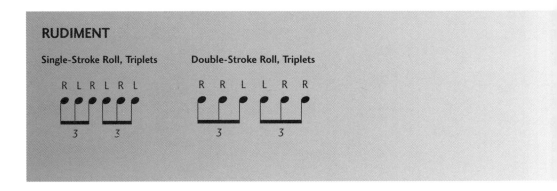

▶ MOVE

The rhythm moves from quarter notes to eighth notes to quarter-note triplets. Different parts of the triplet are orchestrated on the drumset. As in the previous move, the speed at which you can play the bass drum will determine the tempo. Play the whole move from top to bottom.

GROOVE 7. Single-Stroke Roll: Feet and Hands

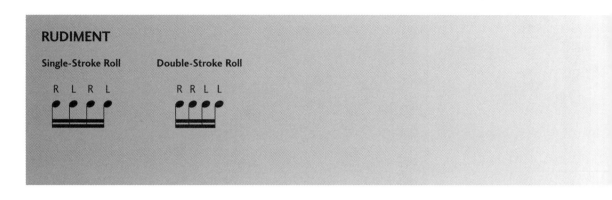

RUDIMENT

Single-Stroke Roll   Double-Stroke Roll

R L R L   R R L L

▶ MOVE 1

The hi-hat foot and bass drum substitute for the hands in this move. On the CD, I play two bars of time, then go into this move.

▶ MOVE 2

The bass drum substitutes for the hands in singles and doubles.

▶ MOVE 3

The bass drum and hi-hat substitute for the hands.

GROOVE 8. Double- and Single-Stroke Roll

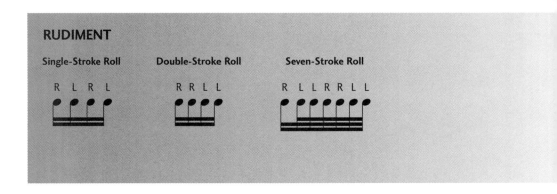

RUDIMENT

Single-Stroke Roll   Double-Stroke Roll   Seven-Stroke Roll

R L R L   R R L L   R L L R R L L

▶ MOVE 1

In this move the hands play double strokes, and the bass drum plays a single. This move may be thought of as a seven-stroke roll.

14

▶ MOVE 2

The hands play double strokes and the bass drum plays a single. This can be thought of as a seven-stroke roll.

15

▶ MOVE 3

The hands and feet play doubles and singles.

16

GROOVE 9. **Double-Stroke Roll**

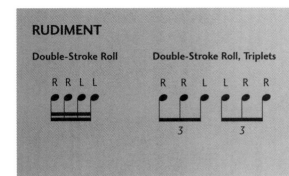

RUDIMENT

Double-Stroke Roll   Double-Stroke Roll, Triplets

R R L L   R R L L R R

▶ MOVE 1

This double-stroke roll is orchestrated on the snare, high tom, and floor tom.
This move can be used as an ostinato (a sustained rhythm) in a groove or as a
solo device. Play with a 6/8 feel. Snares are off.

17

▶ MOVE 2

A double-stroke roll is played as triplets between the floor tom and the high tom.
Orchestrated, this move can be used in soloing.

18

▶ MOVE 3

The bass drum plays the doubles over a triplet-based rhythm to create a 2-bar
phrase.

19

SECTION 3
STROKED ROLL GROOVES

Practice each rudiment on a single drum before trying to orchestrate it on the drum set.

GROOVE 10. **Five-Stroke Roll**

RUDIMENT

Five-Stroke Roll

R R L L R
L L R R L

▶ MOVE 1

This five-stroke roll is orchestrated using a stick-on-stick snare sound. It is played with a jazz feel on the CD example. Use this move as a fill or for soloing.

▶ MOVE 2

This five-stroke roll uses the bass drum playing doubles, and stick-on-stick snare.

▶ MOVE 3

This five-stroke roll combines the ride cymbal into the rudiment. This move can be used while playing time or as a solo device.

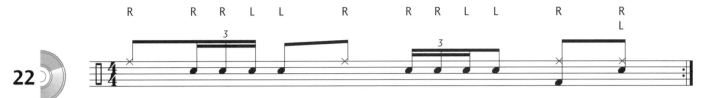

▶ MOVE 4

This five-stroke roll is orchestrated with the ride cymbal. This move can be used while playing time or as a solo idea.

GROOVE 11. Six-Stroke Roll

▶ MOVE 1

In this move, the bass drum doubles the two singles in the six-stroke roll. Use this move as a fill or solo device.

▶ MOVE 2

This six-stroke roll is played within the time. This phrase, if repeated, will be a 3-over-4 phrase, a phrase that continues over the bar line (also referred to as an "over-the-bar-line phrase").

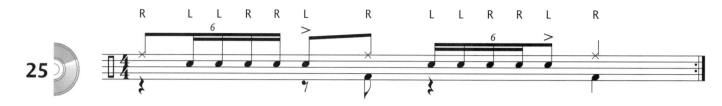

▶ MOVE 3

This over-the-bar-line phrase uses one more triplet grouping and a stick-on-stick snare. This can be used while playing time or in soloing.

▶ MOVE 4a

In moves 4a and 4b, the bass drum plays part of the six-stroke roll. These moves can be used as fills or as solo ideas. They are played in immediate succession on the CD. When repeated, this becomes an over-the-bar-line phrase. Note the stick-on-stick snare.

▶ MOVE 4b

▶ MOVE 5

The right hand plays the hi-hat while the six-stroke roll is played between the snare and bass drum. It can be used in any musical style, and can be a fill or solo idea. Bar 1 and bar 2 are different orchestrations of the same rhythmic phrase.

28

GROOVE 12. Seven-Stroke Roll

RUDIMENT

Seven-Stroke Roll

R   L   L   R   R   L   L

▶ MOVE 1

This is a seven-stroke roll orchestrated on the drum set. It can be used as a fill or as a solo device.

29

▶ MOVE 2

This is a seven-stroke roll between the hands and the bass drum.

30

GROOVE 13. Eleven-Stroke Roll

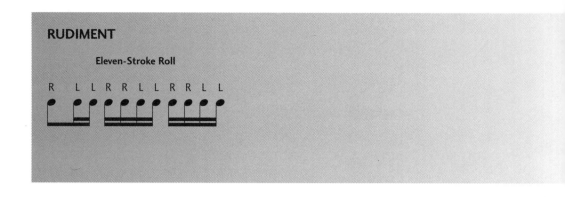

RUDIMENT

Eleven-Stroke Roll

R L L R R L L R R L L

▶ MOVE 1

This is an eleven-stroke roll between the hands and the bass drum. This phrase will go over the bar line.

31

▶ MOVE 2

These are closed rolls or "buzzed" rolls, which are rolls played with multiple bounces. Rolls used this way can be played as a groove over time or as a solo device.

32

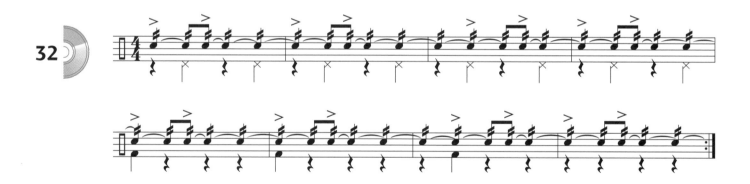

SECTION 4

PARADIDDLE GROOVES

Practice each rudiment on a single drum before trying to orchestrate it on the drum set.

GROOVE 14. Paradiddle Tap

RUDIMENT

Paradiddle Tap

R L R R L

▶ MOVE 1

This phrase will go over the bar line. This move can be used in soloing or over a vamp.

▶ MOVE 2

Another over-the-bar-line phrase. This paradiddle tap utilizes a crossover sticking, with right stick over the left. The crossover is indicated with a "*".

* = Cross over

GROOVE 15. Inverted Paradiddles

RUDIMENT

Inverted Paradiddle

L R R L
R R L R
R L L R
L L R L

▶ MOVE 1

This way of combining two paradiddles can be used in all styles of music, in grooves, and in soloing. The bass drum can be played with the right hand.

▶ MOVE 2

This move substitutes the two left hands from move 1 to the bass drum. Use this as a fill or in soloing.

▶ MOVE 3

This is an inverted paradiddle orchestrated.

GROOVE 16. Inverted Paradiddle Fill

RUDIMENT

Inverted Paradiddle

L R R L
R R L R
R L L R
L L R L

▶ MOVE

This is an inverted paradiddle between the hands and the bass drum. This phrase can be played as written or over the bar line.

GROOVE 17. Paradiddle Groove or Fill

RUDIMENT

Single Paradiddle

L R L L
R L R R

▶ MOVE 1

This paradiddle sets up an over-the-bar-line phrase. The right hand goes from the ride cymbal to the floor tom in this move.

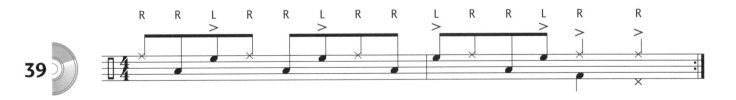

❱ MOVE 2

These are permutations of paradiddles in a 3-over-4, over-the-bar-line phrase.

GROOVE 18. Paradiddle Groove

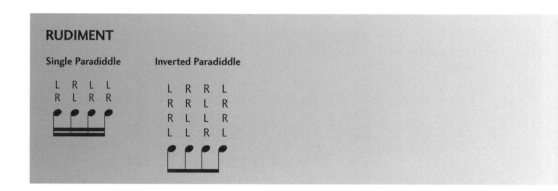

❱ MOVE 1

This move, as played on the CD, shows how paradiddles can be played in grooves in many different styles, depending on the lope (the spin or "flavor") you use.

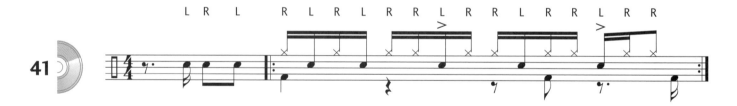

❱ MOVE 2

Here is an inverted paraddidle broken up between the hands and the bass drum. Learn this move first as written, then orchestrate it on the drum set. Play it in any style.

▶ MOVE 3

This is a paradiddle between the snare and the bass drum.

43

GROOVE 19. Paradiddle Groove and Fill

RUDIMENT

Single Paradiddle

```
L R L L
R L R R
```

▶ MOVE 1

This is a groove using combinations of paradiddles. Depending on the feel you play it with, different styles can be implied.

44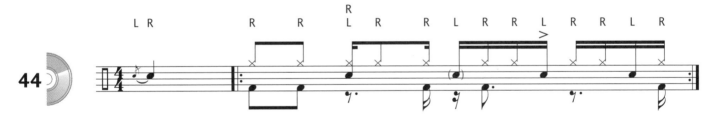

▶ MOVE 2

Here is a fill played within the time, using paradiddles between the snare and bass drum.

45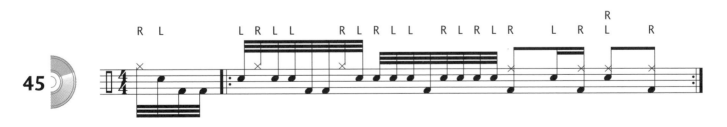

GROOVE 20. Paradiddle Groove

RUDIMENT

Single Paradiddle

```
L   R   L   L
R   L   R   R
```

▶ MOVE

The right hand plays the snare drum and hi-hat paradiddle combinations using sixteenth notes and triplets.

46

GROOVE 21. Paradiddle Groove

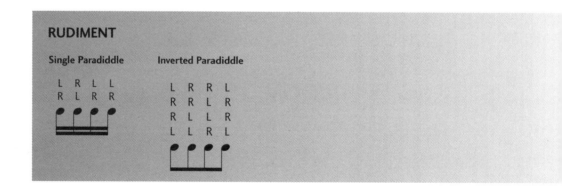

RUDIMENT

Single Paradiddle   Inverted Paradiddle

```
L   R   L   L              L   R   R   L
R   L   R   R              R   R   L   R
                          R   L   L   R
                          L   L   R   L
```

▶ MOVE

These paradiddle combinations create an ostinato pattern when orchestrated on the drums. These can be used while playing time. Snares should be off on this move.

47

GROOVE 22. **Paradiddle Groove**

RUDIMENT

Inverted Paradiddle

```
L   R   R   L
R   R   L   R
R   L   L   R
L   L   R   L
```

▶ MOVE

This move includes a stick shot, in which the right stick strikes the left stick while the left stick is in cross-stick position. This can be used as an ostinato groove or as a solo idea. Snares off on this move.

48

GROOVE 23. **Paradiddle Groove**

RUDIMENT

Inverted Paradiddle

```
L   R   R   L
R   R   L   R
R   L   L   R
L   L   R   L
```

▶ MOVE

This move includes several orchestrated inverted paradiddle combinations. They can be used in soloing or over a vamp. It is a cadential phrase, meaning you can play it with the turnaround. Snares can be on or off on this move.

49

SECTION 5

DOUBLE PARADIDDLE GROOVES

Practice each rudiment on a single drum before trying to orchestrate it on the drum set.

GROOVE 24. Double Paradiddle Groove

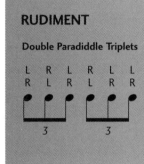

RUDIMENT

Double Paradiddle Triplets

L R L R L L
R L R L R R

▶ MOVE 1

The double paradiddle is orchestrated to outline a 6/8 feel.

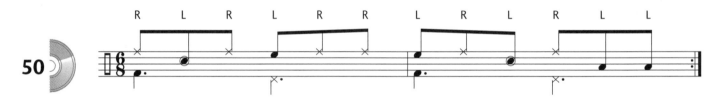

50

▶ MOVE 2

Here are double paradiddles and sextuplets orchestrated on the drum set. This move can be played in 6/8 or in 4/4 time. You can play this cadential phrase and fill with a turnaround.

51

GROOVE 25. Double Paradiddle Fill

RUDIMENT

Double Paradiddle Triplets

▶ MOVE

Here is a double paradiddle between hands and feet orchestrated. It is a 3-over-4, over-the-bar-line phrase.

52

SECTION 6

PARADIDDLE-DIDDLE GROOVES

Practice each rudiment on a single drum before trying to orchestrate it on the drum set.

GROOVE 26. Paradiddle-Diddle Groove

▶ MOVE 1

This is a paradiddle-diddle starting on beat 2 to create a jazz feel.

▶ MOVE 2

The paradiddle-diddle creates a jazz feel, with the hi-hat foot and bass drum creating a 3-over-4 feel.

▶ MOVE 3

A right-hand paradiddle-diddle and a left-hand paradiddle-diddle with the bass drum doubling the right hand. This can be used as an embellishment while playing time or as a solo idea. I play parts A and B together on the CD, but you can use each separately in your drumming.

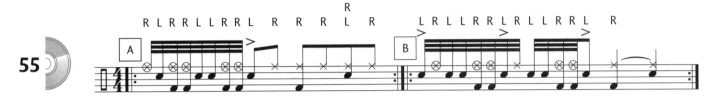

GROOVE 27. Paradiddle-Diddle Groove or Fill

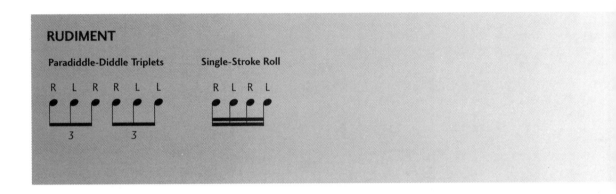

▶ MOVE 1

This paradiddle-diddle and single-stroke roll can be played either within the time or as a solo idea.

▶ MOVE 2

Here's a stick-on-stick idea. The bass drum plays the diddles of the paradiddle-diddles.

GROOVE 28. Paradiddle-Diddle Fills (Plus Three)

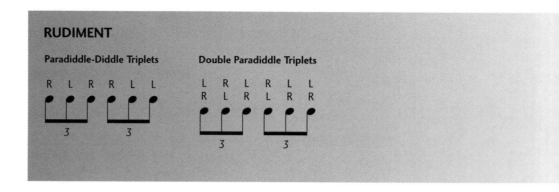

These three moves are "paradiddle-diddle plus three" figures, meaning that in each, I add another group of three (one triplet) to a group of six (two triplets).

▶ MOVE 1

A paradiddle-diddle orchestrated to create a 3-over-4, over-the-bar-line phrase. This move can be used as a cadential phrase.

▶ MOVE 2

The bass drum substitutes for the right hand in the paradiddle-diddles. This move can be used within the time or as a solo idea.

▶ MOVE 3a

A double paradiddle and a paradiddle-diddle orchestrated. This can be used as a cadential phrase.

▶ MOVE 3b

This example starts with the paradiddle-diddle instead of the double paradiddle.

GROOVE 29. Paradiddle-Diddle Fills

▶ MOVE 1

A paradiddle-diddle played on the up-beat.

▶ MOVE 2

This right-hand paradiddle-diddle outlines a 3-over-4 phrase.

SECTION 7

COMBINATIONS OF PARADIDDLES: SINGLE, DOUBLE, AND PARADIDDLE-DIDDLE GROOVES

Practice each rudiment on a single drum before trying to orchestrate it on the drum set.

GROOVE 30. Paradiddle Combinations

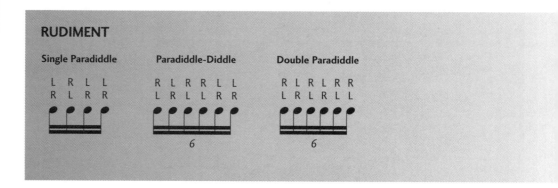

The next four moves are combinations of single paradiddle, paradiddle-diddles, and double paradiddles.

▶ MOVE 1

63

▶ MOVE 2

64

▶ MOVE 3

65

▶ MOVE 4

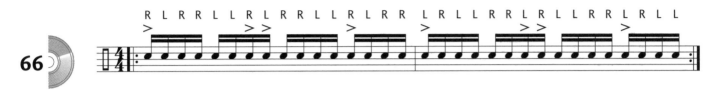

66

SECTION 8

Practice each rudiment on a single drum before trying to orchestrate it on the drum set.

GROOVE 31. Single Ratamacue Groove and Fill

RUDIMENT

Ratamacue

▶ MOVE

This is a single ratamacue to be played within the time.

67

SECTION 9

DRAG GROOVES

Practice drags on a single drum before trying to orchestrate them on the drum set.

GROOVE 32. Single Drag Fill

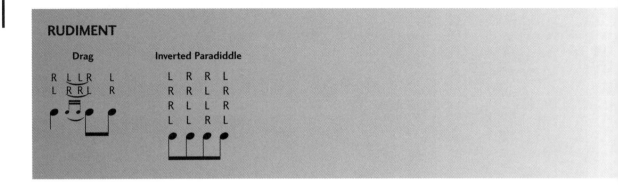

The next two moves are 3-over-4, over-the-bar-line phrases.

▶ MOVE 1

Perform the drags with the left hand.

▶ MOVE 2

At a faster tempo, these inverted paradiddles sound like drags. Play within the time or over a vamp.

GROOVE 33. Single Drag Groove or Fill

▶ MOVE

This is a single drag orchestrated in a 3-over-4 phrase. It can be played on the toms as well.

GROOVE 34. Single Drag Fill

▶ MOVE

Here are single drags between the snare drum and the high tom. The second bar is a 3-over-4 phrase.

GROOVE 35. **Single Drag Groove or Fill**

RUDIMENT

Drag
Ruff

⏵ MOVE

Play this single drag within the time. Also play the open hi-hat part on the ride cymbal.

GROOVE 36. **Single Drag Groove or Fill**

RUDIMENT

Drag

▶ MOVE 1a

Note the stick-on-stick snare.

73

▶ MOVE 1b

This move creates a 3-over-4 phrase if repeated.

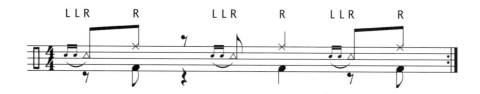

▶ MOVE 2

All snare drum notes are rim shots that can be accented. This move can be used as a solo phrase.

74

SECTION 10

Practice each rudiment on a single drum before trying to orchestrate it on the drum set.

GROOVE 37. Flam Drag Groove and Fill

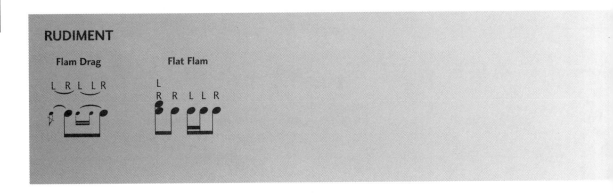

RUDIMENT

Flam Drag

L R L L R

Flat Flam

L
R R L L R

▶ MOVE 1

This move orchestrates flam drags between the high tom and the ride cymbal. It can be used within the time or as a solo idea.

75

▶ MOVE 2

These are "flat" flams, meaning that you play both the right and left sticks together. The right hand "sweeps" up from the floor tom to the snare drum, and the left hand stays on the hi-hat. This is an over-the-bar-line phrase. The drags are on the bass drum.

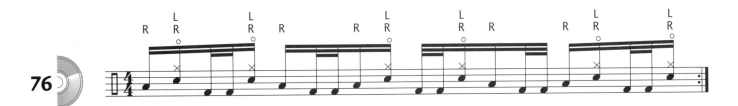

76

GROOVE 38. Flam Triplet Groove

RUDIMENT

Flam Triplet

L R R L

▶ MOVE 1

The right hand comes over to the snare drum from the ride cymbal. Play this move with a shuffle feel.

▶ MOVE 2

This flam triplet moves between the bass drum and the hands. These moves can be used when playing time, as solo ideas, or as cadential phrases. They are stick-on-stick phrases. (Moves A and B are played in immediate succession on the CD.)

▶ MOVE 3

The flam is played by the cross stick being struck by the right hand. This can also be a 3-over-4 phrase.

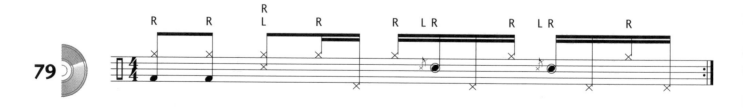

GROOVE 39. Flam Tap Groove and Fill

RUDIMENT

Flam Tap

▶ MOVE

The flam is between the floor tom and the high tom.

GROOVE 40. Swiss Army Triplet or Tap Flam

RUDIMENT

Tap Flam

▶ MOVE

This is a 3-over-4, over-the-bar-line phrase.

SECTION 11
COMBINATION STROKE GROOVES

Practice each rudiment on a single drum before trying to orchestrate it on the drum set.

The hi-hat foot can substitute for one of the stickings of a certain rudiment.

GROOVE 41. Inverted Paradiddle (Hat/Stick)

To create the hat/stick rhythm, the hi-hat is played first with the foot, then the right hand on the closed hi-hat. You then get two hi-hat beats, one using the foot, the next using the hand.

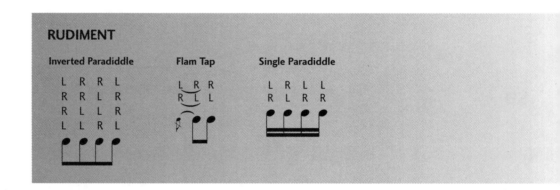

RUDIMENT

Inverted Paradiddle	Flam Tap	Single Paradiddle
L R R L	L R R	L R L L
R R L R	R L L	R L R R
R L L R		
L L R L		

▶ MOVE 1

The hi-hat foot plays the left-hand part of a regular right-handed paradiddle rudiment.

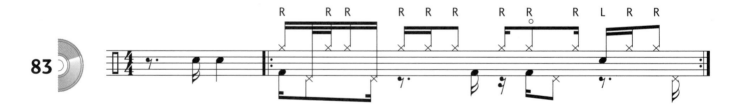

83

▶ MOVE 2

The hi-hat foot plays a part of the inverted paradiddle rudiment.

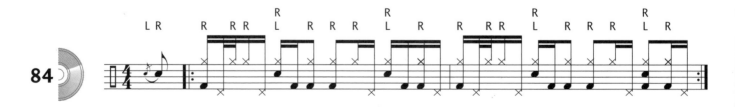

84

38

GROOVE 42. Flam Tap and Five-Stroke Roll

RUDIMENT

Flam Tap   Five-Stroke Roll

▶ MOVE 1

This cadence uses the flam tap and five-stroke roll rudiments to create the groove on the snare and bass drum.

▶ MOVE 2

A snare and bass drum cadence as a groove.

SECTION 12

HAT/STICK GROOVES:
RUDIMENTS USING THE HI-HAT FOOT

Practice each rudiment on a single drum before trying to orchestrate it on the drum set.

GROOVE 43. Ruffs (Hat/Stick)

▶ **MOVE 1**

This move illustrates ruffs as triplets. The hi-hat foot plays the left-hand part of the ruff.

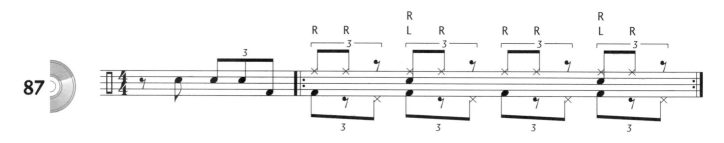

GROOVE 44. Flam Tap or Tap Flam (Hat/Stick)

RUDIMENT

Flam Tap   Tap Flam

▶ MOVE

The left hand moves from hi-hat to snare. The hi-hat foot is the middle note of the triplet.

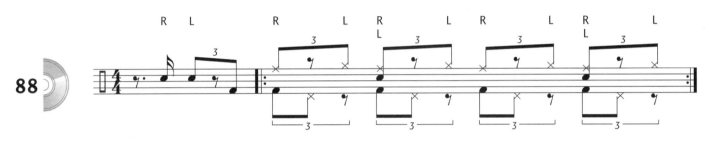

88

GROOVE 45. Paradiddle (Hat/Stick)

RUDIMENT

Single Paradiddle

▶ MOVE

The hi-hat foot plays the left-hand part of the paradiddle.

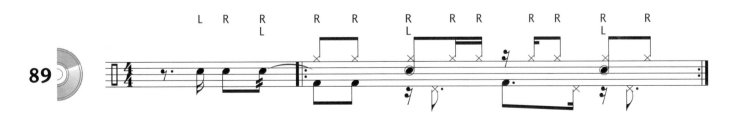

89

GROOVE 46. Inverted Paradiddle (Hat/Stick)

RUDIMENT

Inverted Paradiddle

L R R L
R R L R
R L L R
L L R L

▶ MOVE

The hi-hat foot plays the left-hand part of an inverted paradiddle.

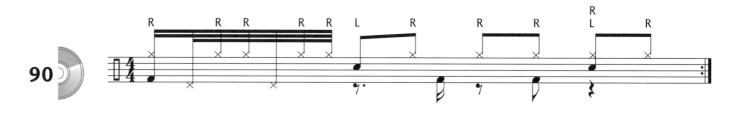

90

GROOVE 47. Drag (Hat/Stick)

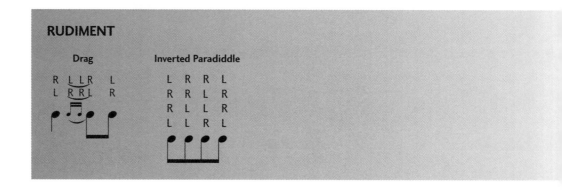

RUDIMENT

Drag

R L L R   L
L R R L   R

Inverted Paradiddle

L R R L
R R L R
R L L R
L L R L

▶ MOVE

This is a combination inverted paradiddle and drag. The right-hand part of the drag is played by the hi-hat foot.

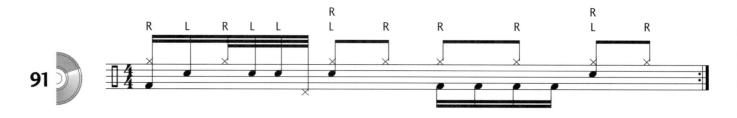

91

GROOVE 48. Drag (Hat/Stick)

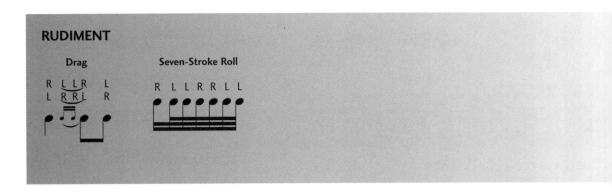

RUDIMENT

Drag

Seven-Stroke Roll

▶ **MOVE**

The hi-hat foot plays a part of the drag and the seven-stroke roll. Vamp on the first or second bar.

92

GROOVE 49. **Ruff, Paradiddle, Single Ratamacue (Hat/Stick)**

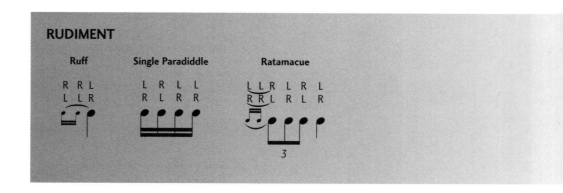

Moves 1, 2, and 3 can be played in succession or separately. (I play them in succession on the CD.) Play each for two to four bars, then go on to the next move.

▶ MOVE 1

The hi-hat foot plays a part of the ruff, single paradiddle, and ratamacue.

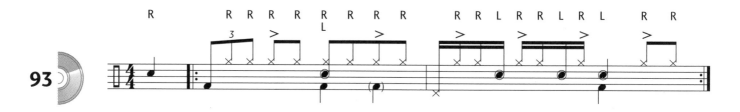

▶ MOVE 2

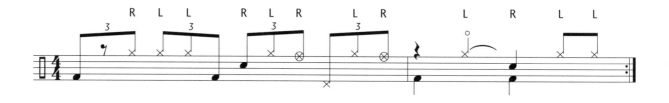

▶ MOVE 3

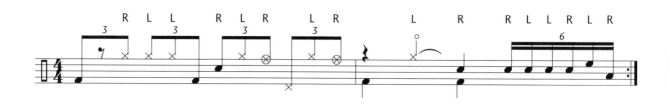

GROOVE 50. Combination Moves

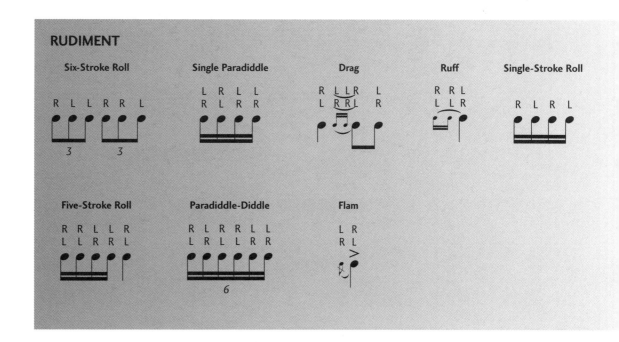

▶ MOVE 1

The bass drum plays a part of the six-stroke roll rudiment. Play a bar of time first, then go into this move.

94

▶ MOVE 2

Play the drags or ruffs between the hi-hat and the snare drum with a single-stroke roll on the bass drum.

95

▶ MOVE 3

This move combines triplets and a paradiddle-diddle at a cadence point. This can be used as an intro or fill.

▶ MOVE 4

A 4-bar fill or a cadential phrase using paradiddles, five-stroke rolls, and para-diddle-diddles, orchestrated.

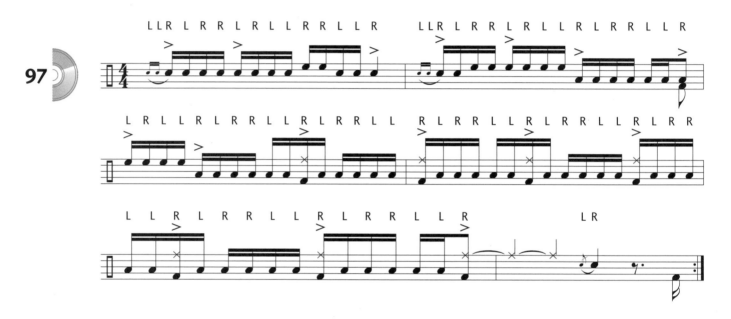

▶ MOVE 5

A 4-bar fill or a cadential phrase using the same rudiments, but orchestrated differently.

CONCLUSION

Each rudiment groove in this book makes its own musical statement. Learning and internalizing each will help you expand your vocabulary to play creative grooves, fills, and solos. Use this book as a starting point—you can orchestrate the rudiments in a virtually infinite number of combinations, in any style, and at any tempo. Your choices of accents, tempos, style, and feel are what will make the rudiments into music.

 Use the rudiment grooves in whatever combinations make sense to you. My solo on track 99 combines all the rudiments used in the book.

GLOSSARY

3-over-4 phrase A phrase that includes two metric feels, as if it were in a "3" feel and a "4" feel. It cannot be completed in a single measure, so it continues over the bar line. Also referred to as an "over-the-bar-line phrase."

Cadential phrase Two or more bars played at the end of a musical form.

Cross rim Left stick rests on drum hoop.

Groove In this book, "groove" is used to refer to a particular rudiment.

Hat/stick The hi-hat is played with the foot and then with the stick.

Move In this book, the "moves" are examples of ways to play the rudiments (or "grooves") on the drum set.

Orchestration To improvise a move on the drum set, playing various parts of the rhythm on the drum set instruments of your choosing.

Ostinato A sustained, repeated pattern that creates a groove.

Rudiments The basic vocabulary of rhythms that drummers arrange and rearrange in various ways in all drumming.

Stick-on-stick Right stick strikes left stick shaft.

Stick-shot Right stick strikes left stick shaft while in cross-rim position.

Turnaround A short harmonic cadence that is used to connect one musical section to another.

Improve Your Groove

with great percussion titles from

Berklee Press

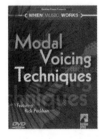

Feed the fire
Career Fuel for working musicians

Berkleemusic.com
Berkleemusic is the new anytime, anywhere online destination where musicians can find jobs and gigs, study with Berklee professors and network with other music industry professionals.

Online music school
Choose from 5 learning streams: **Production, Music Business, Writing, Education** and **Performance**. Designed for musicians, educators and working professionals, courses run from 3 to12 weeks on a six-semester annual calendar.

Music career center
This online crossroads is a 24 by 7 home for monitoring industry buzz, managing personal and professional contacts, finding jobs and gigs, accessing career development tools and networking with like-minded individuals worldwide.

Berklee|*music*.com

Learn more at www.Berkleemusic.com